Empath

By the same author

Emotional Intelligence
Dark Psychology and Manipulation
Emotional Intelligence Mastery

Empath

A Complete Guide for Developing Yourself and Your Gift, Exploring Manipulation, Emotional Intelligence, and Narcissism. Can Everything Be Connected?

Edited by: Judith Dyer

Cover by: Angie

Introduction

We couldn't possibly begin to understand how the first humans perceived each other. They might not have always gotten along, but soon realized the importance of working together to survive. As their brains developed and time went on, they may have found redeeming qualities among one another, especially in reference to mating, as well as understanding the many differences they possessed despite their appearance.

All we have are scientific theories and speculation. It is generally believed (and yet very poorly discussed) that Homo Sapiens ruled over other species of humans because they were fierce and, well, a lot less ethical. These beings saw nothing wrong with eliminating any other species that threatened them for the sake of land ownership and, later on, cultivation (Harari, 2019).

It seems we have always been complex beings, torn between ourselves and our communities, between the different groups we belonged to, and, ultimately, between our physical bodies and moral compass.

There is an excellent reason ancient Greeks encouraged the discovery of our inner selves. The key to a happy life lies beyond the material or social groups, but in how you know and trust yourself. The moment we accept that we are complex creatures that won't ever fit into predefined molds (nor should we want to) is the moment we are set free and can truly embrace our authentic abilities.

The book at hand will discuss just that: being authentic in a world that seems to duplicate personalities like a Xerox machine that works day and night. We know how a "perfect" home should look, and just how many pounds we need to weigh to be considered beautiful in society's eyes. We know how to make the perfect pasta and how to "read" which high school clique to belong to, even though it's been three decades, and doesn't hold power anymore.

We know too little about ourselves. And what's even worse, we know almost nothing about what it means to love the person underneath the facade. When you pertain to typology that is often looked at from extreme perspectives, this makes it even more difficult. Other people will either vilify or glorify you without permission, and little by little, you might start to believe their narrative.

Take empaths, for example. You know how difficult it is to live among people with so many different emotions if you are an empath. You also know, deep inside, that this is a gift, a super-power. Yet, in a society that glorifies the ultra-strong, being sensitive is frequently seen as a weakness or a problem that needs to be fixed, rather than a gift to be embraced.

Empaths come in all the colors of the rainbow. You might pertain to a more extreme category, and you might feel suffocated every time you go out to face a wall of emotions that do not belong to you. You might be a more moderate empath who can function well even in the larger groups.

Wherever you are on this scale, you have likely been told, at least once, that you are *too sensitive*. It might have been a parent, a mentor, your first friend in the world, or your worst enemy. It might have been your abuser, your lover, a coworker, or your boss. Whoever it was, they most likely said it like this is something you need to alter in your personality and way of being.

Well, this book is here to show you the opposite. You do not have to fix your sensitivity. You have to learn how to manage it and how to embrace it as a gift. Empaths can see the world in more colors and flavors that others will never get to experience. They can help so many people; it's almost incredible they are not more celebrated in society. And they can create the kind of art that touches the soul for centuries.

Empaths are truly amazing beings. Unfortunately, they are often those who are the most misunderstood (even by themselves). They are easily hurt and might flip their personality as a result.

To understand an empath, you must first understand the very concept of complexity. Instead of feeling the need to put them into a box with a label, we should take the time to understand this psychological typology as the one that might be our salvation as a species. We need to learn the kindness of an empath and their ability to transcend beyond social norms, religions, and physical borders. We need to embrace our empaths and protect them.

If you are an empath seeking to understand yourself, you should also take the time to understand complexity (and, more specifically, the complex range of emotions you might experience, as well as how easy it is for these emotions to shift towards the negative).

This book will place empaths on its core. As such, we will start off with a chapter designed to offer more information about empaths: what they are, how they are most often defined, the different degrees of the empathy scale, as well as the downsides of being an empath and why it is important to control these pitfalls.

The second chapter will cover acceptance. Learning how to embrace your empathy is extremely important for the development of harmony and happiness as a person - which can be a life-saver for some. As such, we have dedicated a pretty extensive topic on the topic of how you can embrace your typology and make the most out of it.

The third chapter of this book is where things get even more interesting. As mentioned before, people are far too complex to fit into predefined molds. We will debate the intricate relationship between narcissistic personality disorder, empaths, and emotional intelligence as the liaison between the two. As you will see, there is a lot more to empaths and their connection to narcissists than most people believe.

Lastly, we will demystify some of the most common inaccurate things people believe but aren't necessarily true about empaths. As you will read in this last chapter, empaths and narcissists should not always be seen as complete opposites of each other, as their personalities might sometimes intermingle.

This book's primary goal is to help you understand yourself as an empath (if you are one) or someone close to you who is an empath. I believe the key to a better world is by paying attention to how we treat ourselves and each other - and as such, I believe empaths should be empowered with the things they need to make the most out of their talent and help the rest of us connect.

Empaths are one of the most fascinating psychological typologies there is. Distant and frequently socially awkward, empaths are a gift we must all treasure precisely because they possess qualities nobody else has - such as the ability to read between the lines and beyond the appearance of a human being as well as establishing a true kinship.

I hope I can be of real help to you and your loved ones. The information collected in these pages is meant to support further research and self-education, as well as a healthy jump-start into a life-long journey of self-love and gratitude.

Hopefully, by the end, you will know more about yourself, what makes you tick, and how to protect yourself from negative influences and potentially hurtful interactions.

I wish you all the best in this journey of self-discovery, and I genuinely hope it will help you become the best version of yourself. Because, as an empath, you deserve nothing less!

Chapter 1:

What Is an Empath?

Empaths are truly a special breed. They shine a light on the world in a way entirely their own - and for this reason, our society should learn to protect them from negative influences and instead help them grow.

As the term might seem familiar, many people still do not fully understand what an empath is. They might have a vague idea of what empaths are, but they do not know very well how to tell if someone is an empath or not. Sometimes, not even empaths are fully aware of their qualities and the power they hold in their hands.

As such, it only made sense to start this book with a more specific definition of an empath and how to tell if you are one. In the following pages, we take an in-depth look at empathy as a psychological typology and help you understand the importance of knowing your "downsides" as an empath. Once it is clear, we will focus on embracing your empathy and learning how to live with it in a healthy, balanced way.

Without further ado, let's dive into it!

What Are Empaths?

Empaths are people who feel everything the emotions of others and can easily relate to them. They notice the sadness in someone before that person even opens their mouth, and any turbulent thoughts, as well. They are highly tuned to violence, rage, and negative energy. More than that, they absorb all these emotions and take them on as their own because they are not always capable of naturally delimiting between their feelings and what others are experiencing.

In psychology, empathy comes in two main categories: emotional empathy and cognitive empathy. People who fall in the first category can adequately react to whatever someone is experiencing. Those who fall into the second category understand what is happening within others.

In a sense, the empaths I will be mentioning in this book are more likely to fall in the first category. Depending on where exactly on the empathy scale they lie, however, the same empaths can become bearers of cognitive empathy more than emotional compassion. Either way, they are connected by one fact: they can sense the world around them in ways most other people can't.

Empaths are highly sensitive. In the most extreme cases, they will be exposed to the way plants feel and are triggered by violent scenes or anguish in movies. In less severe cases, they are emotional people who absorb the energy of those they interact with (most often, in a way that is unhealthy to both parties of this exchange).

Empaths are great to have as friends because not only will they know how to listen to you in times of trouble, but they will know how to respond to your emotions as if they were going through the same thing. Empaths are exceptional caretakers for the same reason. They are amazing teachers who can easily relate to a younger generation in attempts to spread compassion. They are very frequently vegan or vegetarian, and they have an affinity for animals that few others possess.

In many ways, empaths have supernatural powers. They can sense the world around them and absorb its energy. Naturally, this can prove as an advantage in a multitude of situations. And yet, empaths are not always happy. In fact, they very frequently feel overwhelmed by the entirety of the world. This is mostly related to the fact that they find it very difficult to set a limit between their personal "selves" and those around them. They will indiscriminately absorb whatever comes towards them, positive or negative.

Empaths need time alone and are misunderstood for this reason. It's not that they don't enjoy human interaction - it's just they need this downtime to recharge, and that means setting some "alone" time for themselves.

Sometimes, the issue of being surrounded by people can be so stringent for an empath that they will immediately look to shelter away from crowded places. They might not know anyone in the crowd, but it is likely that they will be overwhelmed by the influx of raw energy around them.

Even when they don't want it, people are naturally inclined to come to an empath to share their problems. This is due to an innate desire to listen, offer advice, and any answers that will feel as if they were a part of that person's soul.

All of these qualities can prove to be a nuisance and a blockade in the growth of an empath. We will discuss the downsides of being an empath in the third section of this chapter. Until then, my suggestion for you is to look over the questionnaire in the following section (as well as read each question's description), and determine where you lie on the empathy scale.

How Empaths Come to Be

Some people are born empaths. They come into the world sensitive and easy to "attack" with everyone else's emotions and energy. Ever since childhood, they find it difficult to handle being around other people - not because they don't like them, but because they intuitively sense that they can be very easily hurt, often unintentionally.

Other people become empaths, as a result of their upbringing and their social and economic context. For instance, someone who was brought up needing love and attention from their parents will be a lot more likely to become extremely sensitive and develop an empathetic character over the course of their lives.

Even more, they are likely to develop other mental health issues, as we will discuss over the course of this book. From depression and anxiety to borderline personality disorder, there is a very wide spectrum of issues empaths can be faced with precisely due to their predilection to being hypersensitive.

There are also empaths who are born in the fire of trauma. Someone who has been through abuse or rape, someone who has gone through critical health issues, or someone who has had extraordinarily difficult times in their lives is more likely to become empathetic (at least) or an empath (at most).

And then there is a very special category of people who become empathetic, but not necessarily embrace the more negative sides of this type of personality too. Empathy is related to emotional intelligence - so if someone works on that, they will manage to become a moderate empath over the course of their lives while completely managing the downsides of their sensitivity to other people's emotions.

Of course, all of this depends on how you choose to understand empaths and their powers. If you want to take a psychological and scientific approach, most people can grow into being empaths to some extent. If you want to take the more spiritual approach, empaths are only *born* that way.

Throughout this book, we will choose to take the middle-way: empaths are neither supernatural beings, nor superheroes. They are not saints, they are not sinners. They are just human beings who, by birth or happenstance, have lost control over how they perceive other people's emotions and energies. In this paradigm, all the downsides of being an empath can be adjusted and managed to help them succeed.

Whichever way you look at it, though, empaths are a gift to the world. They truly have the power to make everyone around them *better* through the prism of how they understand others and how easy they can assimilate their pains and struggles and turn them around.

Are You an Empath?

Empaths almost always "feel" the world around them - but they might not always be aware they are doing this. For an empath, it is natural to feel the emotions and sometimes the physical nature of others. They don't really know how to "deal" with themselves any other way. This is how it's been, and it can come as a shock to learn that the reason they feel a certain way is because of unconsciously absorbing any energy coming their way.

Empaths are very aware of everyone around them, and can sometimes empathize with animals, plants, or environments. Yet, they face the danger of not being aware of themselves - and that is precisely where the trouble can start.

There is no black and white definition of what empathy traits you *must* have to qualify, but here are some of the most common characteristics. As you read, see if you recognize yourself in any of these traits then take the quiz at the end of this section to learn where you are on the empath scale.

Very Sensitive

Empaths are highly sensitive by nature. They are touched by other people's experiences as much as they are by their own. Even more, they tend to absorb art and music at entirely different levels.

Absorbing Other People's Emotions

An empath does not just understand. They really *see* you and feel as you do to the point where they temporarily inherit your experiences.

Introverted

Although there are empaths who feel extroverted (or more likely to be), most of them are introverts. The reason they are frequently closed off is that, for them, introversion is an unconscious mechanism used as protection from the intensity of the outside world.

Intuitive

Empaths have very good intuition. If something doesn't sit well with them, they are more than likely right about whatever it is. Even more, you might not even have to *tell* them something is wrong with you - they will know it either way.

Needing Alone Time

Because they feel so overwhelmed by the wide range of emotions coming at them regularly, most empaths need time alone. This is important to them because it will allow them to recharge their batteries and make it through another day.

Finding Intimate Relationships Overwhelming

Many empaths feel tired after the simplest interactions with other people (even when they don't know them or directly interact with them). When in a relationship, an empath might feel overwhelmed by certain levels of intimacy. A person trying to achieve closeness or instill a connection with an empath might meet a wall that was put up long before that relationship began.

Feeling Energized by Nature

Most empaths connect with nature in ways other people don't. They not only feel more relaxed outdoors, in the stillness of the wild but use this time to charge their internal batteries, finding solace in the beauty of natural landscapes and connecting to them at a very emotional level.

Hypersensitive Senses

An empath's sense of smell, vision, taste, hearing, or touch can be exacerbated. Sometimes, this can go as far as making the empath sick when they smell a certain perfume or fragrance or when someone touches them without permission or who is unfamiliar (especially if they harbor negative energy).

Giving Too Much

Empaths always give too much. They will offer the last piece of food, the little money in their pocket, and an extra hour of their time. As such, they can very frequently forget about themselves - and this can ultimately hurt their self-confidence. In some situations, it might also lead to frustrations for the empath.

Dreading Crowded Places

For an empath, a crowded place like a concert or a mall can feel like a nightmare, because of their tendency to absorb the energy they come into contact with, and a crowded place means an overload.

Inviting People to Open Up

Empaths are very frequently seen as the go-to persons when one needs advice. They are great listeners, and they give sane, emotionally intelligent viewpoints that make them a good shoulder to cry on or someone to vent to without bias.

Avoiding Conflict

There's nothing empaths hate more than conflict. They will go to extreme lengths to avoid disturbing the peace, and sometimes, this might be to their disadvantage.

Feeling Like an Outsider

A lot of (if not most) empaths will feel like they don't fit into most social or group scenarios. This stems from how they always assimilate other people's emotions and energies, as well as from the very fact that they simply see the world in a different light than everyone else around them.

Inability to Set Boundaries

Empaths find it incredibly difficult to set boundaries, and sometimes are unaware of the necessity for these boundaries. We will discuss this more in the next chapter, but for now, it is essential to keep in mind that setting boundaries are crucial for any empath.

A Unique View of the World

Empaths don't just see the world. They sense it with every fiber of their being, in every flavor and fragrance. They see the world through the prism of emotion - both theirs and the people around them.

Easily Connecting with Animals and Babies

Empaths find it easy to connect to animals and babies because they sense a kind of raw honesty that is lost with time and age. The thought of eating meat might actually fill some empaths with horror, as they might feel their food is charged with the energy and the pain of a dying animal - so it's no surprise that many empaths will turn vegan or vegetarian.

Absorbing Physical Pain

Not only do empaths sense emotion - sometimes, they pick up physical pain and illness too. Even more, they might sometimes absorb this pain as their own as well. Naturally, this can lead to a series of issues (as you will see in the following section of this chapter).

Sensing Dishonesty

Because their intuition is heightened, empaths very frequently sense dishonesty or trickery a mile away. Moreover, there's nothing to disappoint an empath more than someone who is insincere to them.

Quiz: Are You an Empath?

Use these questions to help you determine if you are an empath (and where on the empathy scale you might lie). Simply answer the following questions with 'Yes' or 'No,' then total the amount of 'Yes' answers.

1. Do people tell you that you are too sensitive?
2. Do you avoid conflict, even when you are not likely to get directly involved?
3. When you are facing an argument or someone yelling, do you feel physically ill?
4. Does it feel like you never seem to fit in, even when you try (in most social situations or groups)?
5. Do you feel dispirited after being in a crowd?
6. Do you often feel the need to retreat and spend time alone avoiding contact?
7. Do you feel overstimulated when faced with noise, harsh odors, loud sounds, or overly talkative people?
8. Do you have sensitivities to certain fabrics?
9. Do you avoid public transportation and prefer to drive because you can better control your schedule (and avoid crowds)?
10. Do you find yourself eating more when you are stressed out?
11. Do you feel suffocated when you are in an intimate relationship?
12. Are you easy to startle?
13. Do you have any kind of strong reactions to caffeine or medications?
14. Would you say you have a pain threshold lower than the people you know?
15. Are you more tempted to stay isolated, than to socialize?

16. Do you find multitasking to be daunting, tiresome, or overwhelming?
17. Do you feel recharged when you are closer to nature?
18. Have you felt low after dealing with an energy vampire or a person you consider difficult?
19. Do you prefer the countryside or a small town to a large city?
20. Are you more active in one-on-one discussions (usually on deep topics), than in a large group?
21. Do you often find yourself experiencing other people's pain (emotional or even physical)?
22. Do you find violent movies to be extremely disturbing?
23. Do you feel sick if you see someone hurting an animal?
24. Are you a vegan or follow a vegetarian diet?
25. Have you ever found yourself having the same feeling around a specific person?
26. Have you ever noticed your mood instantly changing when someone entered a room?
27. Do you feel confused by your emotions and how rapidly you can switch from one mood to another?
28. Can you influence how other people feel?
29. Do you start talking or behaving like others when you spend a lot of time near them?
30. Do you like being near water (oceans, rivers, lakes)?
31. Do you sometimes feel that you forget about yourself?
32. Do you believe plants and animals have their own consciousness?
33. Are you frequently experiencing feelings of anxiety?
34. Do you find your intuition is almost always right or on course?
35. Do you sometimes feel the energy given out by an inanimate object?

And now, the **results**...

- If you have **less than 5 positive answers**, you are **not an empath**. You might not be the complete opposite, but it is unlikely that you fall under this personality type.
- If you have **between 10 and 15 positive answers,** you are a **moderate empath**. Your intuition is usually very good, and you can easily connect to people. However, you do not always absorb their energies and emotions, and you can set boundaries with relative ease.
- If you have **between 15 and 25 positive answers**, you are a **high-level empath**. You can feel what others feel, you tend to isolate, and you prefer to avoid crowds as often as you can. You are likely the person your friends come to when they need advice or emotional support.
- If you have **more than 25 positive answers**, you are an **extreme empath**. You not only connect to people, you fully absorb their pain and emotions (and often, you can even empathize at a physical level). Even more, you tend to create the same kind of connections with babies, animals, and even inanimate objects.

Keep in mind that this is a self-assessment test and that it might not be entirely accurate. However, it should give you a good idea of where you stand on the empathy scale - and more importantly, it should help you understand yourself more.

The Downsides of Being an Empath

If empaths ruled the world, it would be a much more peaceful place. Yet, empaths are not perfect - and there are plenty of downsides to falling into this psychological category in general. Even more, as you will see in the final chapter of our book, empaths are not always positive, and sometimes can have overwhelmingly negative tendencies.

Nothing is ever either black or white, and you need to understand that there's a myriad of grey shades in between. Empaths are not saints, they are far from perfect, and they too have their shortcomings. Before we get to discuss these darker shades of empathy, I want to take a closer look at the downsides of being an empath.

Losing Your Sense of Self

When you are an empath, and absorb every energy from the people around you, it becomes increasingly easy to lose yourself. In the most extreme cases, empaths cannot distinguish between their emotions and those of the people around them. They offer their help to anyone who needs it and frequently forget to help themselves, which can contribute to them losing their sense of self.

Losing Self-Confidence

As an empath who is constantly troubled by other people's emotions, you might lose your self-confidence too. It's hard to believe in yourself when you don't even know who your "self" is, and this is why empaths might come across as insecure.

Fatigue and Feeling Overwhelmed

Absorbing everyone's moods and emotions can be tiresome. This is especially true with empaths regularly exposed to crowds or empaths who are forced to spend a lot of time around energy vampires, overly talkative people, or in situations where they are forced to go against their nature.

Extensive Solitude

Empaths look for the safety of seclusion and quiet because they cannot handle too much excitement. They find solitude to be comforting and cozy, and they will almost always prefer it to social gatherings of any size. Sometimes, empaths are not naturally antisocial, but in time, seeking solitude is better for them than engaging in too much human interaction.

This can also generate further issues. As solitary people, empaths might be a lot more likely to sink into depression or overwhelming anxiety, and they might find it more difficult to advance from a professional or personal point of view.

Relationship, Intimacy, and Friendship Issues

Because they absorb so much of other people's energies and emotions, empaths tend to find it overwhelming when they find themselves in a relationship. Spending so much time with someone and getting to such a level of intimacy can wear them down. This extends into friendships as well - and is why empaths will be wary when making new friends precisely because getting too close to them can be quite hurtful.

The Occasional Intuition Error

As mentioned before, most empaths have excellent intuition - and as such, they will frequently rely on it, rather than any other raw data type . However, now and then, their intuition can fail them either because of the mixup of emotion or by projecting their own emotions into the situation. When outspoken or taken the wrong way it can lead to stress on the relationship and feelings of doubt to fester.

Overwhelmed by Outside Emotions

Sensing what everyone else senses can look like a superpower when looked at it from afar. In reality, however, it is an intense and draining "activity" empaths have to deal with frequently through the day, often with no warning. It's easy to see how this can be a major downside and how it can lead to severe mental and physical health issues that range from anxiety and depression to chronic pain and other diseases.

Likely to Become a Victim of Abuse

Empaths do one thing better than anyone. They can connect to people, understand, and become part of those people's feelings and emotions. It might sound like a quality we should all possess, but the harsh truth is that sometimes an empath will empathize with the wrong person - such as abusers. This makes empaths very likely to end up as victims of both emotional and physical abuse.

Being an empath is not all sunshine, and it can take you spiraling down on a series of issues that can have serious repercussions. We will discuss this later in the chapter.

Controlling the Downsides

It is quite clear that being an empath has tremendous benefits. At the same time, however, the downsides of being an empath can be life-altering. This is not even a matter of empaths lowering the quality of their life to significant levels.

This is about allowing yourself to live and make the most out of your gift. In the most extreme cases, getting a grip on the downsides of being an empath can be a matter of life and death.

Indeed, knowing *with painful precision* what other people feel can make you a great communicator, an excellent teacher, and a brilliant mentor in your field of expertise. It can make you a remarkable friend, a supportive parent, and an unforgettable lover. With the right training and exercises, it can make you into a great politician, or lawyer; pretty much anything you set your mind to is fair game.

You have to start controlling your negative tendencies because otherwise, you risk falling into a series of mental and physical health issues that will haunt you for the rest of your life.

Depression is common among empaths, not because they are naturally inclined to a more melancholy personality, but because their tendencies are wearing them down. Empaths also favor loneliness more than most, precisely because of issues with proximity. As such, depression becomes even more difficult to handle - and it can very easily become a lot more dangerous as well.

Anxiety in all its shapes and colors is also a common mental health issue empaths frequently find themselves having to deal with. Social anxiety generated by a fear of being worn out by others is common in empaths, but they can easily slip into other forms of stress (including phobias and generalized anxiety disorder).

At a physical level, empaths can feel lethargic and worn out. The act of absorbing emotions that do not belong to them is one that brings them suffering in unusual ways and easily exhausts all of their own feelings and energy.

Chronic fatigue syndrome is a real health issue that can affect empaths precisely because of their weakened state. It can be truly taxing to always feel what everyone else is and to sometimes empathize at levels you do not know how to control.

Why is it important to control the downsides of being an empath?

This is your life, and you cannot afford to waste it in a constant state of inactivity, avoiding people and their emotions, while being unable to fulfill your true goals and dreams because your mind and body are competing with your consciousness. Being an empath can also attract mental and physical health issues through numerous "gateways." As mentioned above, conditions like depression and anxiety are prevalent here.

Because of all your qualities (and how easy they can turn into vulnerabilities), empaths are frequently at risk for ending up in a variety of life situations that don't benefit you or might be considered toxic.

The good news?

You can, without a doubt, gain control of what is going on within your heart. No matter how extreme you think your conditions are, you have the power to control any negative tendencies and create a better life for yourself. And that is what I will cover now.

Chapter 2:

How to Embrace Your Gift

Empaths are like emotional superheroes. Their heightened sensitivity helps them go beyond what people say, and sometimes even beyond what people do. Moreover, their intuition is frequently out of this world, helping them *see* beyond the present and almost predict the future from certain perspectives.

Many of your qualities, even beyond that of an empath, should make you feel proud of who you are. After all, not everyone can say their sensitivity allows them to become another person, if just for a moment or possess the kind of intuition that helps you make educated choices. As shown in the latter half of the previous chapter, this gift has its downsides and some can be extremely serious.

That doesn't mean you should give in to fear and or accept a fate dominated by anxiety, sadness, loneliness, and pain. Like every other psychological trait, yours can be molded to focus on the advantages and help you avoid any obstacles.

This chapter is about helping you embrace your gift because, yes, being an empath should be perceived as nothing less than that. You have a tremendous talent: you can connect to people at levels nobody else can. That makes you one in a million. And in many ways, that makes you the very hope of humanity onwards.

There is true power in emotion, and there is strength in understanding that emotions and empathy are the keys to a world that is a healthy, honest, and a more inspiring place for future generations to thrive.

How do we get there?

Accept Yourself

Fighting nature is not only futile but it can be disastrous. You can't pretend you don't have feelings, and you can't deny that you sense what others feel. You can't lock yourself inside and never allow experiences to come into your life. These characteristics are what define you as an empath.

The best thing to do for yourself, and those around you, is to accept yourself as you are. Social standards might not agree with you and your heightened sense of emotional sensitivity, and some people may find you too much. But that's OK. As an empath, you likely find the "average" person too much for you.

Accepting yourself at your best and your worst is one of the most powerful things you can do for your mental and physical health. It is, in fact, the first step to make towards managing the downsides of being an empath and learning how to live in a balanced way.

Look at yourself and analyze what you see. How are you defined? What characteristics are you proud of? How can you improve the ones you are ashamed of? Be honest, it might be uncomfortable at first and you want to just think about good things. Try to fight that. Look at yourself in the mirror and figuratively strip down to your soul and accept what you see in all its splendor and uniqueness, with the same compassion you show others so frequently.

Trust You

Although empaths tend to have a tremendous intuition (and some even have a very good sense of *what is to come*), they don't always trust themselves. A lack of self-confidence can attract a series of problems in your personal and professional life. At the same time, a lack of self-confidence is not a chronic condition to live with - it can be worked on.

What you have to do first and foremost is start trusting yourself. Have faith in your abilities, trust your knowledge, instincts, and trust your very person. It is a crucial step in embracing yourself as you are and learning how to live beautifully as an empath.

The following are some tips to help you build more self-confidence.

- Spending time by yourself will likely come naturally, but instead of falling into a blackhole of social media content and bad TV, try to find activities that empower the mind, the body, and your understanding of the self. Read beyond the fiction genre, watch documentaries online, exercise, play a sport or practice a form of art. These are great ways to rediscover who you are.
- Set realistic goals. Some people believe that setting insanely high goals will motivate them to work hard and always reach for more. However, that is not entirely true. In fact, setting attainable goals will only make you more likely to make progress. This will reinforce your belief in yourself.
- Build on your strengths. Empaths or not, we all have elements where we excel and where we sometimes fall flat. If you focus on the latter, you will never have the time

(or the energy) to build on the things that set you apart. So, instead of telling yourself, "I can't do this," and make an excuse, start telling yourself, "I can't do this right now, but if I improve...I will be able to..." This is a basic example, but hopefully it shows you how to rewire your thoughts to be beneficial.

- Be kind to you. Indeed, empaths are naturally compassionate to those around them. However, they are not always as understanding when it comes to themselves - making it harder to trust their superpower.
- Be yourself. You might be quirky to some, and insufferable to others. Although your empathic tendencies make you want to be liked by everyone (and less likely to show your true nature), the truth is that you don't owe anyone. Let go of judgment and just be you (even with all the ups and downs).

Love Yourself

For an empath, there is nothing more natural than loving everyone else (and being equally overwhelmed by everyone else's emotions and energy). As odd as it might sound for someone who is not an empath (and has not interacted extensively with one), empaths don't find it just as easy to love themselves.

There are many underlying causes of this. On one hand, empaths are prone to forgetting who they really are. In between trying to make everyone happy and being overloaded with uninvited energy, empaths find it easy to forget about the main priority. As such, empaths can find it quite easy to forget to eat, drink water, or cover basic hygiene. Even more, empaths can find it shockingly easy not to love themselves.

On the other hand, empaths can also grow dark. Most people associate empaths with angelic beings that are thoughtful and forgiving, but the harsh truth is that being an empath can drain you to a point where you become remorseful and bitter. When that happens, an empath might find it even more difficult to find value in their ability. Loving yourself is not an option and empaths need to hear it more often as self-love can act as a shield against waves of negative emotion.

Process Your Energy

Feeling someone else's energy can become problematic in certain situations because it can be hard to distinguish between outside energy. This uncertainty can make you pray for energy vampires. Even if you manage to avoid these kinds of people, as an empath your entire body and mind are an energy hub that never stops working and you are doing it indiscriminately. This can wear down even the toughest soul.

You have to create an energy system that allows you to replenish as often as possible and block out as much external energy as well. Take notes on how much is overwhelming and make sure you continue to do things that help you process your own energy and pain.

When managed correctly, your ability to absorb energy from those around you can help you discover the essence of true self-acceptance. When you learn how to manage the energies coming towards you, as well as those you release, you also learn how to *not have to shut down* and not lash out when you are being triggered.

It takes time to learn how to work with all these concepts, but with the right effort it can make all the difference in the world.

Learn What Troubles You Most

Not all empaths are the same. Some will be triggered by violence in real life or the movies. Others will not be touched by this (they might not like it, but they will not be triggered). Some empaths can be set off by a powerful fragrance, or a certain color. Some will react to vegetation, and others only "deal" with humans.

It is of paramount importance for you to be aware of what troubles you the most. Knowing what your limits are will help you distance yourself from the potential triggers and it will help you better manage the negative side of being an empath.

Same as with learning how to process different energy, learning what triggers you the most can take time. Try keeping a daily journal and mark any troubling or upsetting activity that occurs with your reaction level. Awareness will help you determine the pattern behind all of it (and as such, it will also help you better manage these triggers and how you act).

Remember, we are all different and you might not be triggered by the same things as another empath or simply another human being. That's OK. *You* are the one who has to live with these fears and triggers - so make sure you make your peace with what agitates you and learn how to live with them.

Communicate

Empaths can be excellent communicators (and sometimes they might even naturally lean towards a career in this field). The reason they interact so well is because of their natural listening abilities, and this makes it extremely easy for them to send and receive messages across wavelengths and channels.

And yet, even with the natural-born communication talents empaths possess, they find it difficult to talk about their feelings and what troubles them. They might think others will see them as weak, or don't want to bother someone else with their problems. So these frustrations and energies pile up. Learning how to communicate about the things that bother you is important to progression, as it is the only way to inform those around you what they can do to make you feel better. Speaking up will also help you become more accepting of your personality and this rare typology.

You Are Not a Victim!

Empaths are hurt very easily and sometimes, indirectly. You don't have to intentionally set out to hurt an empath to make them feel bad. Sometimes, they already feel drained and low because of someone else's pain, or they have been around people who emanate negativity.

If you experience this kind of emotion, understand that you are not a victim. Believing this can permanently instill that mentality in your decision-making and subsequent actions. There are only a few steps from this point of thinking and falling under the abuse of someone close to you or succumbing to the pressure you put on yourself.

You are a highly sensitive person who takes things personal, but you can protect yourself from these pains and negative emotions.

You have the power to create shields when they are needed and takedown when you feel that it is right.

You are a warrior who is constantly facing the battle of emotions and energies. You are capable of truly understanding what people feel and think all while coming up with the best solutions to help them.

Practice Deep Breathing

The effectiveness of deep breathing isn't a new concept, but it can help you control your anxiety and your emotions. Studies (Gerritsen, Band, 2018) show that deep breathing is connected to vagus nerve activity. For a bit of background, the vagus nerve is part of the parasympathetic nervous system, regulating the activity of the heart, breathing, and digestion. According to the polyvagal theory (Wagner, 2016), the same nerve is responsible for curbing anxiety, fear, and fight or flight reactions in humans (as a reminiscence of prehistoric times when humanity faced exponential danger every day).

Deep breathing can activate the vagus nerve which activates your body's soothing systems. So, when your heart begins to race and you feel anxious, the vagus nerve will slow things down and bring you back down to a state of rest. Because the vagus nerve is also linked to breathing, it is assumed that slow, controlled breathing can activate the vagus nerve.

These are just a few explanations of how deep breathing can help you control panic or anxiety attacks, as well as a series of reactions you might get when you feel overwhelmed as an empath. While the theoretical explanations of how this exercise works are not conclusive, one thing is for certain, people who practice deep breathing see results.

There is no one correct way to breathe deep and most people will do it instinctually. Try laying down or standing up straight and deeply inhale through the nose using your diaphragm (the top of your stomach). Hold your breath for about ten seconds, and exhale slowly. Repeat for a few minutes or until you feel calm.

Meditate

Meditation is beneficial for empaths because it helps them center, find their core of energy, and distance their emotions from those of other people. In itself, meditation is both a deep breathing exercise and an exercise of the mind. It helps you take control of your thoughts and use your body to train a reliable support system you can call upon when needed.

There are many types of meditation, and most of them bring a similar range of benefits:

- Reduce stress levels
- Help with anxiety management
- Strengthen emotional health
- Help fight addictions
- Help manage depression
- Reduce age-related loss of memory
- Help you be kinder and more compassionate.

The most common types of meditation include:

- Progressive relaxation involves slowly relaxing different parts of the body with soothing music or candles and sometimes under the guidance of a recording or another person. This type of meditation will help you focus on your breath and your body. As such, it will help you release stress and anxiety and find your center of balance as well.
- Kundalini yoga. At the crossroads between yoga and meditation, Kundalini yoga focuses on releasing the Kundalini energy (located at the base of the spine). To achieve that, you will have to practice some poses, combined with deep breathing and mantras. It is the same as progressive relaxation, Kundalini yoga helps you get a hold of your thoughts and your anxiety and train your body.
- Zen meditation is perhaps the most common image you get when you think of seated contemplation. It involves sitting still with your legs crossed (or in the lotus position) and focusing inwards. Most times, this is done by

counting deep breaths and trying to eliminate all rogue thoughts.

- Transcendental meditation. This type of meditation is quite similar to Zen meditation, with the main difference is its purpose to transcend beyond the material. It involves a mantra and that can be focused on every time a different thought slips into your consciousness. Very frequently, transcendental meditation is connected to spiritual and religious ceremonies. Some types of prayers in Christianity are considered forms of transcendental meditation (such as rosary beads prayers, for example).
- Guided meditation. This is often done either under the guidance of a therapist or under the guidance of a recording (YouTube, audiobooks, or even DIY recordings for those with experience). Sometimes, guided meditation and progressive relaxation meditation are combined.

Not all types of meditation are suitable for everyone, and that's more than OK. It is generally recommended to try out as many options as you can to determine which suits you the best.

Center Yourself

Centering yourself is something you have to do as an empath. It can help many types of people, indeed, but it tends to be particularly helpful in the case of empaths because it creates distance between the emotions of others and allows them to focus on *themselves*.

Centering yourself is also known as *grounding*, precisely because the exercises and techniques meant to help you with this are based on bringing you inwards and helping you move past the constant and uncontrollable absorption of energies and emotions that do not belong to you.

There are multiple ways to ground yourself, here are a few practices to get you started:

- Exercise. Working out is an act of focus, first and foremost. When you exercise, it's just you and your body (even if you participate in group classes, for example). Furthermore, exercising helps you learn how to control your body in a different way while retaining focus. It enables you to ground yourself in the moment and truly allow yourself to just *be*, despite what is going on around you. In addition to all this, exercising is health for the body and the mind - so it is the best thing you can do for yourself.
- Take a bath. Long hot baths are a great way to unwind after a long or exceptionally testing day. Add bath salts or oils to match your mood, and your baths will become more than just a luxury - allow it to calm your state of mind, feel how you feel in that moment and detach yourself from the outside world.
- Spend time in nature. As we were saying before, empaths are naturally drawn to nature and wide open spaces. Trekking down a new path in your favorite park or strolling on the beach can help you get closer to *you* by achieving clarity and peace of mind.
- Play. It could be a video game, a board game, or simply something childish you do on your own. Whatever it is, though, simply allow yourself to *be* in the purest and most innocently foolish way. The whole point is to allow yourself to be a kid, however that might translate to you.
- Have sex. In many ways, sex is both a mental and a physical exercise, as it allows you to release tension,

relieve stress, and reconnect to your body. Sex is a healthy activity (not to mention *quite* pleasurable)!

- Arts and crafts. Practicing any form of arts and crafts is a great way to reconnect to your inner self. You don't have to worry about it being "artistic" or even aesthetic, though. Just play around. Choose your medium and your materials and allow your inner artist to go wild. Painting, sculpting, knitting - do whatever suits you best!

- Restful sleep. This might sound like the most basic tip, but the truth is that it can make a world of difference. Getting eight to nine hours of sleep every night and keeping it consistent will revitalize your day. Uninterrupted sleep hours allow your body to be healthy and your mind to stay focused and detached at the same time.

- Avoid addictive substances. Alcohol might seem like a temporary refuge for empaths who feel overwhelmed or want to interact with other people without feeling overwhelmed with outside emotions that do not pertain to them. However, this is just another escape, a shortcut to taking responsibilities or things you feel out of your control. Excessive use of alcohol can be hazardous for your long term physical health and will throw off any progress you've made with your mentality. Avoid using substances as a way to feel numb, and you will be able to stay grounded and focus on the things that matter.

- Practice affirmations. This might not be for everyone, but some people swear by this habit. Saying positive affirmations in the mirror or when you wake up can help you focus on what matters for you and it can help center yourself as the day progresses.

Some examples of affirmations empaths could use include the following:

- "I promise to honor my sensitivity and treat myself kindly."
- "I promise to explore my empathic gifts and make the most out of them."
- "I will communicate about my sensitivity with those around me, for this is the best way to protect myself and others."
- "I will make the most out of my sensitivities to become better for myself and those around me."

- Read for fun. Reading is not only a great way to escape stress, the mundane, and the pain of having to absorb everyone else's suffering and emotions, but they are a great way to practice your focus and your cognitive abilities. In turn, this will also help you ground easier when you need it and return to a neutral state, instead of continuously attracting other people's energies.
- Journaling. Prompt-based journaling can help you (re)discover yourself and create a healthier mindset. Basically, prompt-based journaling means writing in a journal based on different prompts such as a happy memory of your childhood, a moment when your empathic nature hurt you, or a moment when you made someone else's day better.

  Prompt-based journaling can help you learn more about who you truly are, which, in turn, will also help you ground yourself and disconnect from others when necessary. If you don't like the idea of prompt-based journaling, you can just try writing freely in a journal, as regularly as you can - it will still help a lot.

  If prompt-based journaling does not suit you, that is completely fine, as there are other types of journaling available out there too. For example, these ones are quite popular:

53

- Bullet journaling (used for organizing plans and ideas, as well as track moods, for example).
- Dream journaling (where you add your dreams in a journal; this is particularly useful for those empaths who might have troubling recurring dreams, for example).
- Goal journaling (where you write about your goals and what you are doing to achieve them).
- Free journaling (where you just write about your feelings).
- Gratitude journaling (where you write about things that make you feel grateful; sometimes, this type of journaling is combined with prompt-based journaling).

These are just some methods you can use to ground yourself. Remember, everyone is different, so you might not find all these ideas to work for you. It's OK to feel that something is not right for your particular situation or lifestyle, try something new or make it into something all your own. There is no exact science on how to do this the right way; you are the only one who can reshape your life from here, so try out these methods, see what suits you, and go with it.

Call Upon Your Spiritual Shields

Same as some of the grounding techniques presented in the previous section, this specific method of embracing your empathy and learning how to live with it might not be for everyone.

If you are a spiritual person, it might be worth giving it a try, as many empaths are quite happy with the results. This involves choosing a person or an animal you can mentally call upon when you feel rushed by other people's emotions. Everyone does this differently, but most empaths choose to say a mantra that helps them regain control and feel protected.

For instance, your spiritual shield might be a lion. When you feel overwhelmed, you could say something along the lines of "I call the lion, my spiritual protector to be here with me and shield me from the negativity."

Release Negative Energy

The easiest way to release bad energy is by replacing it with something positive. Anytime you feel overwhelmed by negativity (or a wave of negative emotions from an outside source), think of how you can turn it around and make it a positive experience. For instance, if you have to attend a party and you don't feel exactly entirely sure how this scenario will play out, instead of lingering on all of the ways it can go wrong instead think of the positive outcomes of branching out. Calling a friend you cherish to join you in support can also lighten the anxiety.

Don't allow harmful energy to pile up in your mind and your soul. Most of the techniques we described in the section dedicated to grounding yourself can be used to release tension. Again, try each one and see what you like best - it is the only way to find out what truly works for you.

Set Boundaries

Setting boundaries can be extremely difficult for empaths, for reasons that are easy to understand if you are one or if you live with one. Setting confines comes naturally to most people as a way of protection or creating a bubble around themselves. However, in the case of empaths, this can be difficult when you are regularly distracted by feelings of the outside world and forget about your own well-being.

It sounds odd for someone who has never had to face this kind of problem, not only do empaths find it hard to set boundaries, but they may not understand or feel comfortable with the concept. And yet, boundaries can save you from being swept into a sea of emotions and energy that are not yours, precisely because they set a figurative bubble around your senses and your body and allow you to function normally.

How to do this? Here are some important tips:

1. Recognize and name your limits. As we were saying before, taking the time to know yourself and what you (don't) like is important. Boundaries are directly influenced by how much you know yourself, precisely because knowing what bothers you means you can *name it* and *fully recognize it* in both yourself and others.
2. Be straightforward. You might feel like you are hurting someone's feelings if you just tell them that you are not OK with something they are doing. However, chances are they will be happier knowing what irritates you so they can avoid doing it in the future. Be polite and kind but always straightforward. Simply tell them you do not feel comfortable when they do something.
3. Let go of fear and guilt. Not only are these the biggest roadblocks on the path to success of any kind, but they will prevent you from setting healthy boundaries. When you are afraid to say how you feel because you think it will hurt people or if you feel guilty for expressing what they did that bothers you, you are dismissing your own feelings in place of theirs. That habit only stunts growth.

4. Put yourself first. It might be the hardest thing to do for an empath, but it is an absolute necessity. Prioritize yourself before you prioritize others. If you want to, compare this to the instructions you get on an airplane: in case of something going wrong, you are supposed to put on *your* mask first and then help the person sitting next to you. You can keep on helping others if you don't help yourself!

5. Don't be afraid to ask for help. Counseling and support groups can help you understand why you have such a big problem with setting boundaries. Furthermore, they can give you the strength to start doing this for yourself.

6. Follow through with your statements. If you have told someone you are not OK with them doing something, make sure you remind them if they keep on doing it. Assertiveness is seldom a quality of empaths, but it is one they can build, little by little with time.

7. Start small. You don't have to set big boundaries from the very beginning. Start small, with telling your co-worker when you don't like an insensitive joke or want to gossip about others in the workplace.

Accepting who you are is not always easy - especially in the case of empaths. It takes hard work and conscious practice to manage the least advantageous characteristics of your personality and typology. Once you do, however, you open the gates to so much more. These are not just random encouraging words to boost ego, they are the facts at the foundation of success.

Chapter 3:

Manipulation, Emotional Intelligence,

and Narcissism

Empaths have to deal with a lot each day they step out their door, but if there is something that needs to be discussed, that is the manipulation and narcissistic manipulators, as well as their relation to empaths.

Many people tend to see empaths and narcissists as complete opposites, but the truth might be surprising. In this chapter, we will look at the primary connection between narcissists and empaths, as well as the bridging topic that brings them together, emotional intelligence.

As you know, nothing in is ever *black* or *white* - and people make no exception. Empaths are skilled, but when they lose control, they can become a source of negative energy themselves. Likewise, narcissists are not evil; they can be as pleasant as the next person, if not more.

It is essential to read between the lines and distinguish the difference between empaths and narcissists, as well as the relationship that seems to connect them like complementary parts of the same whole.

Let's explore this deep connection between manipulation, narcissists, empaths, and emotional intelligence.

What Is a Narcissist?

Narcissism is more than just a type of personality. From a psychological perspective, narcissism is believed to be a disorder.

To understand this personality disorder, we go back to the very origin of the word, Narcissus, a major name within Greek mythology. There are multiple versions of this story, but the most common depicts Narcissus as a very handsome man. One day a mountain nymph named Echo sees him and falls in love. She follows him through the forest and reveals her identity to him, he cruelly denies her and tells her to go away. She then lives out the rest of her life pining after him until she turns into nothing.

Learning of what Narcissus had done, Nemesis, the goddess of revenge, punishes him by bewitching him to fall in love with his own reflection. This is where multiple versions of the story cross. Some say Narcissus lived in pain, realizing that his love for himself would never be reciprocated. Others say Narcissus committed suicide. In typical Greek fashion, his end is tragic as a result of his dark fate.

Narcissistic personality disorder came into light at the beginning of the 20th century, and it is considered a difficult condition to treat with therapy because patients tend to be unresponsive or bothered by their behavior. Most narcissists do not believe they have an actual problem because, as you will see later in this section, narcissists only see themselves as the epicenter of the world. So it is easy to understand why they would be more than reluctant to consider changing or even admitting they have a problem.

On top of that, narcissists tend to be quite disconnected from other people in a way that seems opposite of empaths. Their disorder most times does not make *them* suffer as much as it makes everyone else around them suffer until, like the nymph in the story, they vanish into nothing but a shadow of what they were.

A narcissist can consume you the same way fire consumes everything in its way. Because of their charm and alluring nature, you are bound to be attracted to them one way or another. Like fire, they shine bright and warm; they are bubbly and unique, look attractive, and know their way around the heart. Yet, instead of making you happy, they will find a way to absorb your energy until you have nothing left.

Narcissistic Characteristics

Everyone has narcissistic characteristics, but to be clinically diagnosed with narcissistic personality disorder (NPD), you need more than just a grandiose sense of self-importance or a budding influencer career. Sure, there might be people who share these tendencies, but just because someone is overly interested in their appearance, it does not necessarily mean they have a disorder.

The "true" narcissists tend to take this to new extremes. Think of a self-centered person and multiply that by 10 or 20 - that's when you get a narcissist in the clinical and psychological sense of the word.

So, what are the characteristics or symptoms of someone with NPD?

- They have a tremendous sense of self-importance. They might just seem confident at first, but the severity of the self-interest will eventually reveal an infatuation. They are the most important people in the world as far as they are concerned, the *centrum mundi* or center around which everyone else lives.
- They have delusions of grandeur, most times associated with a fantasy life that pertains to them only. Most of the time, narcissists see themselves with only impressive skills and excel at everything they enjoy. When the world around them fails to comply with their sense of self they very easily retreat into a world of pure fantasy that keeps on feeding their megalomania.
- They require constant praise and admiration. Everyone likes to feel admired, but narcissists take it to a new level. They might even react wildly if they don't get their way. For them, there is nothing more important than

appearing a certain way in front of others, either flaunting their looks, education, upbringing, or other social aspects.

- They have an acute sense of entitlement. Narcissists believe they deserve everything under the Sun, and more. As such, they will never accept a "no" from anyone, nor will they accept the fact that not everything is owed to them (and that not everyone has to do as they please).
- They exploit other people without any kind of remorse. They will always take what they need from others, and sometimes they will even use manipulation to get it. Once they achieve their goals, however, don't expect remorse.
- They are natural bullies picking on people; usually, those they consider weaker than them, using harsh or cruel names, and might lash out with violence.
- They expect special treatment. Narcissists want everyone to treat them special because they genuinely believe they *are* above everyone else. As such, they deserve special treatment in a variety of situations ranging from work to their personal life.
- They never recognize anyone else's needs or desires. Narcissists are the exact opposite of empaths in this respect because they do not listen; they simply do not care about others or their emotions and needs. The narcissist's needs and desires will always come before anyone else's, even when it is someone close to them.
- They feed themselves with greed. Narcissists are very often envious of other people's happiness and success. In their turn, they *live* to make other people jealous as well.
- They come across as conceited. When you see a narcissist for the first time, they are perceived as overly confident (at the very least) and downright arrogant.
- They always want *the best* (in everything and of everything). Narcissists will never accept second place. They believe they are supposed to be the best at everything: at work, and even in love (which is why they

will often manipulate their partner and tear them away from their friends and family).

- They overreact when they don't have the advantage. Narcissists can get incredibly violent when things don't turn out a certain way - and this is precisely why they are likely to become emotionally or physically abusive.
- They find it more than difficult to manage stress or change. Although a narcissist will take pride in knowing how to handle a wide range of situations, the truth is that they don't. Their low self-confidence, and impatience make them react poorly when faced with adversity, stress, or life changes. Most often, they will place the blame on anyone else but themselves.
- They are sometimes moody and depressed because they do not achieve absolute perfection. Narcissists are the absolute perfectionists, but since perfection often falls short of reach for them, they will often get depressed or moody when they see things haven't gone exactly how they planned them to.
- They usually hide a lot of fear and insecurity. The harsh truth is that all of it is a facade. Deep inside, they are insecure, anxious, and most of the things they do and say are meant to cover that up. Sometimes, not even they are fully aware of just how insecure they feel, precisely because they have learned to fake it so well that they eventually fool themselves.

We are complex beings, and it would be impossible to fit every narcissist into the same mold. The vast majority of times, people who suffer from NPD will either inhibit just some of the characteristics described above or display them to some degree.

Unfortunately, many times narcissists can become abusers - and very often, the abuse is directed at empathic people. They might be abusers to a lesser extent or slip into the deep end and become physically abusive.

Even so, it is extremely important to not look at a narcissist as plain evil. Nobody is inherently evil. Indeed, narcissists are more likely to do things that are unethical, immoral, and downright mean - but it is essential for you and for them to understand that matters can sometimes be gray. rather than black and white.

When a narcissist realizes the effect they have on people and when they actually want to change, therapy is available. Most narcissists do not walk this path, as we will discuss further on. However, those who do can, indeed, find their balance.

This is not to say someone should remain in a relationship with a narcissist, hoping they will change. Most times, they don't. However, looking at this in a biased way will do neither of you any good. Understand that narcissistic personality disorder is complex and can affect you and the person suffering in different ways.

A Narcissist's Effect on Others

Narcissists are almost born to make others feel bad. They suck out energy, take advantage of weaknesses, and show little to no remorse in the process. If they are allowed to have it their way, narcissists can do the same things to those close to them over and over again.

It is almost impossible to live with or near a narcissist and not be affected in some way. If you are an empath, there's an even bigger chance that you will be altered by the emotionally and potentially physically abusive behaviors of a narcissist - precisely because you feel bad and want to help them, as they continue to take everything away from you.

Just like the nymph, you might end up a shadow of what you used to be. Your entire life and personality could be absorbed by the narcissistic behavior of the person next to you - and yet, you might still want to empathize with them.

People who live with someone displaying this degree of selfish behavior encounter depression from being picked on and feel nothing they ever do is good enough. These people fall into a continuous cycle of abuse. The only person who can pick them up is the abuser and it can go on forever.

Anxiety, low self-confidence, pain, anger, depression are just some of the mental health issues people living next to an abusive narcissist can experience. In time, they end up losing themselves, and even the will to live.

In terms of physical health, a narcissistic abuser can inflict a lot of actual physical damage, especially when they become physically violent. To understand the extent at which this can go, think about this: in the United States, more than 50 women are shot by their intimate partner (n.a, 2019) every year. And keep in mind that this statistic only includes those who die by shooting. Some fall prey to beatings, others suffer irreparable physical damage, and others end up with incurable diseases.

The numbers cannot fully encompass the range of effects a narcissistic abuser can have on those around them. Even more, statistics often fail to include emotional abuse effects as well, as it is virtually impossible to measure the extent of mental and emotional suffering these victims have to put up with.

Living with a narcissist might not always lead to physical abuse. And sometimes, it might not even display the most extreme case scenarios in terms of emotional abuse either. Even so, a narcissist's influence on those around them can be terrifying. As such, it is of the utmost importance for both ends of these relationships to take action.

As sad as it might be, in the vast majority of cases, *leaving* is the only real solution. Disconnecting from the narcissist's actions and influence and starting anew is the only way to fully regain your power, energy, and in the worst case, your will to live.

Bear in mind: the same effects (and the same ultimate solution) can appear in the case of people who are near a narcissist, but not necessarily in a romantic relationship with them. Narcissists can abuse their friends, parents, siblings, employees, coworkers, and spread toxicity in whatever room they inhabit.

A Narcissist's Effect on Themselves

A narcissist's effect on others is, without a doubt, tremendous.

Not many people consider the actual effect a narcissist can have on themselves (since they are often vilified). It would be unfair to our premise (nothing being one way or the other) not to consider the kind of effect narcissistic behavior can have on the person exhibiting it. On the outside, everything can look more than fine. Narcissists have made it their goal to hide insecurities, anxiety, and any flaws that would suggest imperfection. Covering it in a layer of false self-confidence and so-called "social success."

In reality, there is a battle raging inside the narcissist. They *know* they are not well. The very fact that their perfectionist tendencies make them likely to develop symptoms of depression goes to show that what they are doing impacts their own life as well.

Despite knowing, narcissists will only rarely ask for help. Yes, therapy is helpful and medication that has been proven to show results in preventing delusions and manic tendencies. But to get to that point the narcissist must admit they need help.

They don't do this, though. Most of the time relying on what they think are suitable "treatments." They keep on feeding their egos and false beliefs that do not match reality. They hang on to fantasies with every ounce of strength, and in the process bring everyone else down with them. Eventually, narcissists end up displaying severe self-destructive behavior. Their disorder eats them alive, and just like with fire, they burn away.

Protecting Yourself from a Narcissist

Most people do not actually realize when they are around a person displaying narcissistic behavior especially when first meeting.

Narcissists can be really striking. Usually the type that lays on the charm, wit, and intelligence. They mimic affection like no other, and will shower you with attention or gifts. They can even look and act as if they really care about you. Narcissists are excellent at attracting people into their web, precisely because they know they need other people to make it. You need to know the signs of narcissistic personality disorder, since appearances can be deceptive.

Here are some of the things you should look for:

- They are always right. You stand no chance to antagonize them in any way. If they voice an opinion, you can't talk them out of it.

- They never apologize. No matter how many mistakes they might make, and no matter how many times they do it you won't hear an admission of guilt. And when they do apologize, it will be a non-apology and it will be obvious they don't mean it (notice the pattern continuing even after the apology).
- They gaslight you (e.g. it feels like they are turning you into a different person, like you are always crazy, you are always wrong, you constantly have to apologize even when you are not at fault, and so on).
- They pick on you all the time. They call you names, constantly annoy you for the fun of it, or become aggressive.
- They do not want to define your relationship. If you are dating a narcissist, you might notice that they refuse to admit you are in a relationship because they "cant" commit.
- They lack empathy at a very high degree. Some narcissists might show empathy in very specific situations, but the majority of the time they will be the complete opposite of compassionate.
- They tend not to have long-term friends. One of the first things you might notice is that narcissists do not have many long-term friends (or even *no* long-term friends). They have either been left behind due to their behavior or used their friends for as long as they needed before discarding them.
- They always ask for compliments and *feed* off of them. A narcissist LOVES admiration, even if it is fake and their inflated sense of self will be fueled by positive reinforcement.
- They will constantly interrupt you even if it's a very important or serious topic. Notice they always talk about themselves and their skills or change the conversation towards the discussion of them. Since narcissists do not

care about the people around them, they will often interrupt anyone speaking in small groups when they get bored to refocus the attention on them.

You can protect yourself from these people by picking up on the signs described above. It is important to see the red flags and try to stay as objective as you can when making an assessment. Keep in mind a narcissist will be extremely charming so it might be difficult at first to read them. Even more, try asking them about some of the things that might be red flags, they will more than likely shut down this line of questions. They can use their aloof nature to do this, or be evasive. In addition to knowing the signs, it is also good to know how to set boundaries. If you are an empath, you might find this difficult to do, as we discussed in Chapter two.

You can use small steps like these to make a big difference in protecting yourself from a narcissist:

- Ignoring them when they display conceited or self-centered behavior
- Not taking the bait and refusing to engage in a fight
- Understanding that their criticism is not actually about you
- Using clear communication with them
- Trusting your intuition and your feelings about them
- Always remind yourself that you are worthy of kindness, compassion, and affection.

Ultimately, the single most important and most efficient way to avoid the negative influence of a narcissist is to *stay away*. If you decide to remove yourself, be confident and stick to your guns no matter how much they protest. Odds are that you have given them one too many chances already anyway, so there's a pretty low possibility that they will actually change (even if they say they will). We will discuss this matter in a little more detail in the last section of this chapter.

Life with a narcissist can be incredibly difficult, regardless of whether it is a life partner, parent, or friend. You have the power to walk away from any situation that is no longer serving you, regain control, and never look back.

What Is Emotional Intelligence?

Intelligence can be defined in many ways. For a long time, most people believed that IQ (intelligence quotient) measures how smart a person is - but in recent times, we have all come to realize that "intelligence" as a whole cannot be defined by one such parameter.

Indeed, testing your IQ can show that you are good with math and seeing patterns, but there is a lot more to humans than just that. The first humans evolved because they were able to see patterns and create tools and mechanisms that helped them survive in a world full of dangers.

Beyond that, however, humans have always exhibited signs of other types of intelligence. Cave paintings are a clear sign that ever since our beginnings, we always wanted to show our emotions. More than that, we wanted to show we were *there*.

Intelligence cannot and should absolutely not be defined by only one vertical. If that were true and we were to actually judge the value of a human being based on their IQ alone, most of the serial killers and murdering psychopaths in history would be at the top of the list.

Emotional intelligence is a relatively new concept, developed only towards the second half of the 20th century. Although quite young, emotional intelligence is now considered to be a measurable and valid way to measure a person's capacities.

Emotional intelligence does not deal with math problems and patterns, though, but with a human being's capacity to understand their own emotions and those of others, as well as distinguish between the different types of emotions, their different shades, and the degrees at which they can affect a person.

Emotional intelligence comes under multiple names such as "emotional quotient" or "emotional leadership and can be narrowed down to a handful of elements. According to Daniel Goleman (Mindtools, n.d.), there are five basic elements of emotional intelligence:

- self-awareness
- self-regulation
- motivation
- empathy
- social skills

Despite what some people might believe, there are numerous implications to emotional intelligence. This is not about having healthy love relationships only; it's about being a more than just "functional" human being and, in the end achieving success (however you define it). For example, some companies will use EQ as a prediction of job performance, and prefer emotional intelligence levels over references.

It makes sense if you think of it. Emotional intelligence is a cumulus of traits (as mentioned above), and all of them can help you become more successful. People who are more emotionally intelligent are also more likely to be more motivated, more resilient, and more hard-working. They can also communicate more efficiently, they can manage stress better, and they can be reasoned with in easier ways as well.

The same qualities can be transferred to any area of life. A person who has a high degree of emotional intelligence will know how to respect their partner. They will know how to understand their emotions. Even more, they will not flee at the first sign of trouble either, precisely because they are used to being resilient.

The best news about all of this is that emotional intelligence can be improved. There are many things you can do to "train" your EQ muscles, and most of these things focus on the five components of emotional intelligence shown above.

More specifically, here are some tips you want to keep in mind:

- Learn how to communicate assertively. It will help you set clear boundaries, but it will also make sure there is no room for interpretation. Clearly and politely state your wishes, needs, and opinions. It will not hurt those around you, but it will provide them with a set of guidelines to follow when they interact with you.
- Respond, don't react. When it comes to conflict, most of us *react* before we attempt to address the problem. It's a lot more natural to defend yourself and lash out at someone who has wronged you, but it is not always the best course of action. So, instead of allowing yourself to explore further and fuel the conflict, address the problems in a mature and strategic way. Conflicts happen, but they can also be resolved when you treat matters in a healthy way.
- Practice active listening. A lot of people believe communication is all about what you say. However, efficient communication is approximately 75% about listening (which is exactly what most people fail at). If you

want to be a great communicator, learn how to listen first. Focus on the other person and what they are saying instead of deciding how to respond.

- Motivate yourself. Motivation is a large part of emotional intelligence, so it is important to work on it as well. Keep in mind that "motivation" has nothing to do with unattainable goals, as much as it has to do with how you work with your inner self. Set goals that are specific, clear, and realistic, stay on track by following through with your plan and remind yourself why you are doing this.
- Focus on a positive attitude. Negativity has a way of creeping into your bones and shadowing your entire life. Not only can it make you feel less hopeful and less likely to feel motivated, but it can also affect your mental and physical health. It can lower your emotional intelligence and slowly shift your focus from the entire range of emotions to just the dark ones.
- Practice journaling. This is a simple exercise you can pick up if you want to become more self-aware and want to get to the bottom of certain behaviors you might display. For example, prompt-based journaling can help you find topics to write about, but more importantly, it can help you find topics to examine within yourself (such as fond memories or times when you managed to do something great for yourself).
- Work out. Good for the body, exercising helps you relieve stress, focus on what matters, and regain control over your emotions. Exercising is one of the healthiest habits you can pick up and the best part is it doesn't really matter *what* type of workout you choose (as long as it makes you move, get your heart rate up and sweat, it's good for you).
- Learn how to be more self-aware. There are many ways to do this. Meditation can also help you become more aware of your thoughts and your body. Yoga, prayer, or slow

walks around the park. Do what makes you feel good and helps you turn inwards. That's how genuine self-awareness is born.

- Accept feedback and criticism. Nobody is perfect, and knowing how to receive critical feedback and analysis is actually a sign of a sturdy emotional intelligence. Keep in mind that it may not be about you as much as it is about the person addressing you, so learn how to "filter" the feedback you get based on who is emitting it, the circumstances, and your relationship.

- Walk a mile in someone else's shoes. The greatest way to empathize with someone is to simply try to see what they see and think about what they think. For an empath, this is the most natural thing in the world. For the rest, it might take a bit of practice, but it can be done.

- Be sociable, friendly, and approachable. Humans are social animals, and our survival as a species is due to our ability to come together and protect each other. Being friendly and approachable is not about survival anymore, but it can make you a more understanding person. It can also make you more likely to understand different types of people and how they *feel*.

- Accept it when it is your fault and hold yourself accountable. Knowing when to hold yourself accountable is a sign of emotional maturity and intelligence - so do learn how to do it. It is important to be balanced about it, but what is perhaps even more important is making sure that it's not based on simply *blaming* yourself. Taking responsibility for your actions also means that you take responsibility for the changes you will want to enact here on.

- Find an inner balance. Being calmed and contained is a sign of emotional intelligence as well. In general, self-awareness helps people be calmer even in situations that would otherwise turn them on fire - so practice exercises that help you become more self-aware and relax your mind and body.

- Pay more attention to body language. Communication is not always about the words only. Someone can say they are OK, but their hands, their eyes, and the very way they hold their head up (or not) can say the complete opposite. Pay attention to body language. You might not need a dictionary for it, but knowing how to read people can help ease communication and increase empathy. And remember to pay attention to your body language!
- Respond to other people's feelings. If you feel someone is not OK with something you said or did, make sure to address it maturely and calmly. Communication is key!

Of course, it would be nearly impossible to encompass everything emotional intelligence is in just a couple of pages. What you do have to keep in mind is that emotional intelligence is the bridge of communication between people who might seem opposite and yes, that includes empaths and narcissists as well.

Emotional intelligence is also a muscle you can grow. The more you listen, the more you empathize, and the more you know how to turn inwards when that is needed, you will likely reap all the benefits that come with a high level of emotional intelligence:

- Become a better team player and leader
- Achieve your personal and professional goals
- Manage stress and change in healthier ways
- Learn how to read people and how to interact with them

Yes, you can train your emotional intelligence muscle! You just have to want it!

Empaths, Narcissists, and Emotional Intelligence

As shown in the previous section, emotional intelligence is quintessential to being not only a morally just and figuratively good person, but a crucial element in defining success (if not through any other perspective, then through that of motivation).

Empaths and narcissists are somewhat at the different poles of emotional intelligence but empaths at least poses one of the five elements. They might lack in other areas such as self-awareness, self-regulation, and even basic social skills. In these cases empaths completely remove themselves from social activity for the simple fact that proximity to other humans *hurts* them.

On the other end of the spectrum, narcissists possess little to no empathy. However, they are often very motivated, and many times possess the kind of social skills that make them likable in many respects.

Both empaths and narcissists lack self-awareness. Empaths are not aware of where their emotions and the emotions of others begin, while narcissists are not aware that they should be considerate of other people's feelings at all (or even think it's a problem).

Furthermore, both empaths and narcissists lack self-regulation. An empath will find it extremely difficult to auto-regulate their emotions in a healthy way. The only way they feel natural when faced with an avalanche of energy is to retreat in themselves, which might not always be the healthiest way to deal with things. On the other hand, narcissists do not self-regulate because, in their opinion, they do not need to. They are so perfect in their mind that they don't feel the need to change.

As opposing as they might seem, empaths and narcissists are frequently drawn to each other in ways that might feel almost inexplicable. Empaths will find the "brokenness" of a narcissist to be a life-long goal. They will try to attend to or "fix" them with endless understanding and little to no honest, blunt communication about the things that are truly wrong with their behavior.

Narcissists will be drawn to empaths because of the way they stimulate their ego. Empaths will offer praise, allow them to express themselves and essentially do what they want, and always give them what they need.

In the end, narcissists will consume the empath's energy, and the empath will grow bitter, resentful, or depressed. If nothing changes and if their behaviors remain the same, they will burn away and fall into despair without being fully able to disconnect from their toxic relationship.

You see this often: relationships that are clearly broken or toxic and based entirely on codependency and feeding into each other's most negative traits. It could be an intimate relationship, a relationship between parent and child or friendships as well.

Until one of the partners makes a step to set boundaries, nothing will change, and things will only escalate into disaster. Most often, these boundaries have to be physical and the two will have to separate.

From the outside, leaving this kind of relationship is the most natural thing to do. From the inside, however, it is a much more difficult and complex step. Statistics show that three-quarters of the women who die at the hands of a loved one are killed *after* leaving the relationship (Kasperkevic, 2014).

Of course, these numbers are not meant to scare you or make you stay in an abusive relationship for the sake of safety. Rather than that, they are meant to help you understand the situation and be prepared. We will discuss more about leaving abusive relationships in the following section of this chapter, though - so stay tuned if you are interested in that.

This is largely due to the sometimes violent nature of a narcissist who is left unexpectedly by the one person they never thought would leave. Not getting their daily dose of praise or feeling cared for can leave them empty and uncontrollable that they might default into completely irresponsible behavior. Murder is one of them, but some abusers stalk their former partners to the point where it all grows to be a scenario torn out of thriller movies.

Empathy and narcissism are two sides of the same coin. Both lack self-confidence and feel completely inopportune in the world around them. They are very frequently drawn to each other because at some stage, they offer each other exactly what they need: understanding and charm. As the relationship evolves, they might even find themselves at each other's throat for the same reason that brought them together: their unique nature.

The relationship between an empath and a narcissist does not always have to end tragically, but it will end most of the time. The old adage "opposites attract" might seem romantic or fit into movie plots, but in real life it can lead to an impasse that pendulates between love and hate, codependency and obsession, remorse and regret.

In the last chapter of our book, we will explore the tight-knit relationship between empaths and narcissists through a different light. Most times, they are on opposite sides, but the truth might have a wider spectrum than many professionals realize.

Leaving Narcissistic Abuse as An Empath

If you are an empath (or anyone else) in a narcissistic abusive relationship, you have to find a way out. You might try to understand the person next to you and you might want with all your heart to make sense of the situation. However, more often than not, these problems only escalate.

When it comes to this situation and this type of person it's best to have a plan. You have to be very careful about how you plan as well, especially since a narcissistic abuser can very easily stalk and stomp on your plans and make the situation worse for you.

Some of the most important tips to keep in mind include:

- Ask for help. Talk to someone about what you are going through. It might be hard, you might feel ashamed, and you might not even feel like you have the power to talk about it. However, you have to. Ask for the support of your friends and family - and if you have none left or none you can call for, do ask for the support of specialized organizations.
- If you research ways to leave or find a support group online, make sure you do it securely, in a way that will not let your partner find out what you are doing.
- Always have a bag with necessities ready. Include your paperwork, essential clothing and items you can't live without and have it well-hidden and within reach in case you need to leave in a rush.
- Plan ahead. Save some money, maybe even try to set up a place for you to live for a while after leaving the relationship.

- Cut them off completely. A narcissistic abuser will want to take you back. They will promise to change, they will be extremely nice with you, and they might even go as far as stalk you or follow you around to ask them to come back. Make sure you cut all ties with them and never look back. It is for your good and for *their* good as well.
- Be strong. This is especially true if you are an empath, but it can be applied to everyone else as well. When leaving an abusive relationship, you will most likely feel as if you are leaving behind your favorite drug. Narcissists are very good at making *them* your drug - so do expect to feel weakened and to want to come back, just as you would when quitting any kind of addictive substance.
- You don't have to have the talk with them. There is a high chance that they will grow angry at you - and even if there might not have been physical abuse until then, you might still have to face it now.
- Leave as far away as you can. If possible, choose to live with someone for a while - a friend or a family member, for example. It might disrupt your life, but it will also keep you safe (and less likely to consider going back).

Leaving a narcissistic abuser is in no way easy. However, it is the only way to make sure you extract yourself from the toxic situation and heal. Things might escalate (as they frequently do), things might stay the same. Either way, there is little chance that the abuser will change under your influence. And there is even less of a chance that things will ever get better in the full sense of the word.

Be brave and do this for yourself. You need it, and whether you realize it or not, your partner needs it as well. You are not doing yourself any good, nor are you helping them by staying and feeding into the toxicity.

Leaving is, unfortunately, the only solution in the vast majority of cases. The main exception from the rule is when the abuser realizes their behavior and is ready to get help. And only if they are making an active effort to follow through with their promises and displaying consistently improved behavior.

Healthy Narcissism: The Right Amount

Most people believe narcissism is bad - and, as we have shown it throughout this chapter it can, indeed, get *pretty* nasty (especially through the perspective of how they can influence other people's lives).

We also said narcissism is not *evil*, and that is true as well. It might sound contradictory, but as we will discuss in Chapter 4, things are rarely *this* or *that* - most often, they are in the middle.

The "middle" of narcissism has a name: healthy narcissism. The term is used by psychologists to describe a healthy amount of self-confidence and finding joy in your own person.

Children usually develop narcissistic traits starting with the age of two when they also begin to use words like "I," "mine," and "no," (you will see this exemplified the best in how children may not be so willing to share their toys with others).

As some people grow older, they tend to go to either of the extremes: too narcissistic or not narcissistic at all. Finding a balance between the two will help you be more self-confident in general - and thus, enjoy life and the fruit of your labor.

The main differences between someone who is a narcissist and someone who has just the right amount of narcissism in them lie in:

- Quietness. Healthy narcissists do not need to be loud or even vocal about their self-confidence.
- Their behavior towards other people. Healthy narcissists will not move past certain limits and they will not hurt others with an exacerbated sense of self-confidence. They will respect others just as much as they respect themselves.
- Working well with others. Healthy narcissists know how to be a team player, and the importance of working together towards a common goal, whereas narcissists rarely do.
- Not always needing approval or validation. Healthy narcissists do not ask for approvals and compliments, they earn them.
- Flexibility. Someone who has a healthy amount of narcissism will always be flexible, especially towards other people's needs. Narcissists are almost never flexible.

There is nothing wrong with emphasizing your good qualities, as long as you don't solely focus on them. As such, developing healthy narcissism can help people (including empaths) believe in themselves and be more successful.

Chapter 4:

Myths and Misunderstandings: Empathic Narcissists, Manipulation, and EQ

After reading thus far, you might feel that the very term empathic narcissist is an oxymoron or a very bad joke. But it is a special category that lingers between the two - a type that is as odd as it is real, as fascinating as it can be painful.

How is this possible?

It's Never Black or White

Books published and the movies we watch have broken our perception of the world. The bad guys in the movies are almost entirely bad, and the good guys are always superheroes ready to save the day no matter the harm it inflicts upon themselves.

Life isn't a fairytale with incapable princesses, scary ogres, and princes lined up to save the day. That would make life far too easy. You would spot the bad guy from a mile away and run like hell.

In real life, "bad" guys are the dashing and attractive ones, laying on the charm and quick wit. Even more, like everything else under the Sun, they are not entirely bad. Even more, good guys are not always cut out to be a Prince Charming in terms of how they look and treat others. At the end of the day, they too have their flaws (some of which might seem appalling).

Things are never black and white, and the relationship between narcissism and empathy isn't either. It would be easy to vilify the narcissist and make him/her a perpetual predator, but the complexity of the human mind prevents us from categorizing people in simplistic, fairytale-like terms. Right?

Empaths are no saints, either. As you will see in this chapter, they can become vain, self-centered, and extraordinarily mean. But they also hurt deeply.

Someone who is a narcissist can be conscious of other people's emotions. They might semi-consciously choose not to be, though, because it suits them and their purpose. Likewise, someone who is an empath might not actively perceive everyone else's emotions and they are not all mind readers.

Both empaths and narcissists are introverts by nature (but the narcissist will have taught themselves how to appear open and extroverted). They both focus in unhealthy ways - the empath retreats into themselves and pushes everyone else away. The narcissist does it by attracting everyone else towards themselves and shutting down inside at the slightest sign of emotional connection.

Learning how to see the spectrum is precisely what gives people a higher level of emotional intelligence. Fairy tales are fine for children learning how to tell right from wrong but as an adult, you should try to see beyond the black and white scenarios and understand that human beings are entirely too complex to fit into molds.

Empathic Narcissists

If you put matters into perspective and take into account the many layers of a person you will quickly understand there is nothing absurd about the concept of an empathic narcissist.

What are some of this typology's traits? Do you notice any similarities?

- They oscillate between acting superior and feeling hurt when they are attacked (directly or not).
- They feel entirely separate from everyone else. And as such, deserve different treatment.
- They are quite offended by criticism (even when it is not actually real).
- They seldom take responsibility for their actions but are quick to cast the blame.
- Their personal affairs almost always consume them.
- They manipulate and control those around them through self-martyrdom (always posing as the victim in every situation).
- They think nobody can understand them.
- They always feel like a victim of other people (or even the world itself).
- They always see other people in extremes (they are either amazing or evil, either angels or demons).
- There are few options when it comes to beliefs, social conditioning, or mindsets that differ from the ones they were raised with.

An empathic narcissist can be a vegetarian who won't ever understand why they sacrifice animals in some cultures. It might be a person of a higher social status not understanding how the

88

less fortunate do not allow themselves to grow. It is a person who doesn't think eating organic is an option for a family of six dependent on single income.

Empathic narcissists might look pure from afar, but they are frequently very self-centered and only care about themselves and their immediate outcome. These types are the most common compared to just narcissistic or empathic (to some degree, as long as it is not an extreme case). They hide in plain sight and they can sway either way without any kind of difficulty. They can pose as saviors and saints, but they can also be conceited and narrow-minded, unable to truly process other people's emotions and backgrounds.

Can Empaths Be Manipulative?

Most people think empaths are almost always the ones who are manipulated, but there is a special category of empaths that can learn how to manipulate as well. This happens with empaths who has been involved with a narcissist in the past. It can take years before they fully internalize the fact that they are abused but when they do, they can use their intuitive nature to turn a narcissist's behavior against them.

Yes, empaths can be manipulative. Even if we exclude the more extreme cases like the one described in the paragraph above, empaths can use their ability to read emotions to their advantage.

As we were saying earlier in the book, people aren't "saints", and empaths are no exception from this rule. This is not to say that all empaths are manipulative, but some can become extremely cunning, and use their sensitivity in other ways.

Do Empaths Have a High EQ?

Emotional intelligence or emotional quotient (EQ) is a mark of a person's capacity to understand others and themselves, as well as clearly distinguish emotions and act accordingly.

As a general rule, we are tempted to believe that empaths are naturally gifted with a very high EQ. Moreover, many people believe that those with high EQ must be empathic. Neither statement is true. Empaths might have a high EQ, but not always. Likewise, someone who has a high EQ might not be sensitive to other people's emotions (on the contrary, those with a really high EQ will know where to draw the line between emotions and priorities).

Emotional intelligence tends to be misunderstood because most people associate it with empathy in its purest form. However, as shown in the previous chapter, EQ is defined by five elements. As we were saying there, empaths excel in one of these areas, but frequently lack or are neutrally mediocre in others. As such, it would be incorrect to assume all empaths have a high emotional intelligence (there is a good chance they are more emotionally intelligent than most people who don't "train" themselves, but it is not a mandatory concept).

Likewise, it would be incorrect to say narcissists themselves have low EQ. They can be extremely smart from an emotional point of view. Even more, they can display characteristics that might even seem compassionate when it's necessary or benefits them. It's just that they very commonly choose not to (and this choice might be more or less conscious).

Clearly, both narcissists and empaths are still shrouded in mystery and misunderstanding. If we had to narrow down this entire book to one takeaway, it would be this: people are complex and so are their situations. Never judge a book or a relationship by its cover and learn how to take the best course of action for your own wellness.

Balance is the key. Learn how to move past appearances (even if that's what draws you in). Learn how to disconnect and tune in to yourself. Embrace the imperfections, pay attention to what your gut is telling you, and keep learning.

Because you are. And you deserve nothing less than the very best in life!

Borderline Personality Disorder and Empaths

A lack of emotional control characterizes borderline personality disorder (BPD). There are nine symptoms associated with BPD and the people who suffer from it, namely:

- Fear of abandonment
- Strings of unstable or toxic relationships
- An unclear self-image
- Self-destructive behaviors
- Self-harm (or suicidal behaviors)
- Extreme emotional shifts
- Consistent feelings of emptiness
- Uncontrollable anger
- Feeling out of touch with reality

At first glance, this disorder may not seem to have much to do with empathy. However, studies have shown that people who suffer from borderline personality disorder are a lot more likely to display extremely high levels of empathy.

There are quite a lot of pieces of research in this direction, including functional magnetic resonance imaging studies that show a higher level of empathy (Flasbeck, Enzi, Brüne, 2019). They show that empathy and this condition are connected not only by perspectives or professional opinions, but by physiology.

Empaths and people who suffer from borderline personality disorder seem to be intrinsically linked and this relates to the very way in which these issues develop in early childhood. Some are just born empathic, while others develop high levels of empathy as they grow more conscious. Higher sensitivity associated with empathy, makes it possible to develop BPD as they are constantly faced with mood swings influenced by external factors.

As you have seen in the third and fourth chapters of this book, empathy is not all rainbows, not through the perspective of those who suffer under it, and if you ask those that witness the behavior. Empathy has its own dark side and it is important for both empaths and their loved ones to be on the lookout for these negative tendencies.

When looking at empathy and its less-than-positive sides, look at BPD and how the two connect, it can be the key to truly understanding dark empaths and their inclinations.

- The capacity to read people without really knowing them.
- An incapacity to navigate social situations alone.
- A tendency to become depressed because of the emotions they experience.
- Using self-harm as an escape.
- Violent mood swings.

Not all BPD patients are highly empathetic, and this must be emphasized. However, a lot of empaths might sooner or later develop the negative symptoms of this condition as well (Lo, 2018).

This will help you gain a broader understanding of what empaths go through and just how dangerous it is for them to not manage their negative tendencies. Borderline personality disorder is not easy to deal with, and if an empath decides to go into therapy, it is important for them to acknowledge potential adjacent issues.

Having a 360 view of behaviors and emotions is so important in the process of healing!

Conclusion

If we stopped labeling people, the world would be a better place. No matter how hard we try to get away from self-imposed clichés, it seems they always come crawling back.

Since the birth of conscious thought, humans have been inclined to put people into one category or another, because let's face it, the unknown can be frightening. Some were hunters and gatherers, others stayed in the hearth and helped grow the community. Eventually, we paired off, our group numbers dwindled, and those hunters became farmers, while others protected the family, perpetuating all the way to the present day. Our roles may have changed, but the mentality has stayed the same.

Being an empath is more than just a psychological category. It is a label, most times. For the vast majority of people, it's a label that carries the sting of "failure in a world that values the rich, the powerful, and the insensitive."

Things don't have to be this way, though. Empaths do not need to stand in line to find compassion from the other people if they are fountains of acceptance. They do not have to be social pariahs.

If you are an empath, you should be proud of yourself. Being an empath is a label that bears uniqueness. Like a priceless work of art, you are here to make the world more dynamic, beautiful, and filled with color.

You have the power to do whatever you want to do. You can be an amazing leader, a successful entrepreneur, a renowned actor or artist, a bubbly socialite, or a truly amazing mother or father. Design your own life. Although it might not seem like it, you have an ability to *sense* things others miss and you can use this to your advantage.

Obviously, this is not an encouragement for manipulation. More than anything, it is one of the *many* examples of how empaths can use their talent to create greatness in the world. If more empaths learned how to control the downsides that darken their lives, this entire planet would be greener, happier, and most definitely a lot more compassionate toward those who need it the most.

Understanding that your empath" label is not a sentence to a life lived secluded and away from other people's energies and emotions is the beginning of a journey you will definitely love.

You might feel anxiety when faced with the bigger picture and want to reject society's standards, and you can do that. But imagine having the tools to step into the role you're meant to play.

Being an empath can be overwhelming. It can hurt, physically and emotionally. It can take you down and it can take everything away from you precisely because you allow yourself to be a victim to people who do nothing but...take.

Being an empath can bring you to the brink of despair in a multitude of situations. From having to be surrounded by too many people every day to having to live your life near a narcissistic abuser, there are many circumstances in this world that can completely break you. Someone who is not an empath might find it easier to extract themselves from these situations - but as an empath, you might find it a lot more difficult.

It's complicated, and might sometimes earn you the label of manipulation. In the most extreme cases, it might even associate you with your exact opposite: a narcissist. But such is being human. Nobody is all good or all bad, and as an empath, you are no exception. The key lies isn't about sweeping your defects under the rug, but learning what they are and how to manage so you can avoid hurting others.

This book has taken you from the most basic definition of an empath to the complexities of sub-categories such as empathic narcissists and manipulative empaths. I hope this has helped you understand just how intricate humans are and how important it is for everyone to accept themselves as they are. To look at themselves naked in the mirror and embrace the painful parts instead of covering them up with false self-confidence the way narcissists do.

Deep inside, narcissists are hurt. It's almost incredible that there's an underlying soft interior. Many have experienced traumatic childhoods or some form of abuse. Many have built up a shell and retreated into a delusional world with themselves as the center.

Narcissists are not evil, and it is important for everyone to understand. That does not mean you should remain a captive in a relationship that does not serve you with endless cycles of abuse and instant gratification. It just means that you have to accept the reality that you cannot help someone who won't admit they have a problem or rejects help. And that is what a narcissist will do, again and again.

In a world that puts celebrity and golden shines on pedestals and forgets about what makes us truly human (imperfection, that is), being sensitive might be perceived as a flaw.

Throughout history, we choose to remember those who fought for humankind and knew the importance of understanding each other through a perspective of compassion and love. We also remember those who did the opposite.

When German industrialist Oskar Schindler took advantage of a legislation bracket to offer jobs (and thus, *save* from death) more than 1,200 of Jewish people, he did it through a perspective of compassion. We truly treasure Schindler's attitude because we know his nemesis and how his positive actions were born.

Gustav Klimt's painting, *The Kiss*, is another great example that shows just how thirsty the world is for kindness and beauty. A painting that portrays a man and a woman embracing and kissing each other, all revealed in warm shades of gold, *The Kiss* is famous everywhere in the world. We all adore its delicacy and the way it portrays the disintegration of someone in the arms of the one they love. That is precisely why we keep coming back to it, again, and again.

Ultimately, we pay to go to the movies because they make us feel something.

We are sold models of perfection, power, and emotional distance everyday. Yet, deep inside, all we want are real emotions, feelings, in all their rawness, beauty, and to experience the raw power of transformation for a better life.

Empaths are amazing humans because they understand the best we have to give even if we aren't willing to admit it. We might have a dark history, and our survival as a species is based on acts of terror and blood-shed. Deep inside, though, all we have ever worked for is being close to each other, loving one another, and having the ability to express it.

As an empath, you have the power to contribute to a whole new world of peace and love. Hippies might have dreamed of it, but we now have the information and the data you need to lift yourself up, take control of your emotions, and make the most out of your genuine talent.

Hopefully, this book has helped you understand how to embrace your being as it is and how to protect yourself from those negative influences that can truly take you down. More than anything, I genuinely hope this book has taught you something very important about true self-love: it is the key to changing the world.

I wish you all the very best in your future endeavors, and I hope the information I have provided will be a boost into a whole new version of yourself, the one you were born to be, the BEST!

Author Note

Thank you for reading one of my books! This is the third book I've written since 2019. It took me years to decide to write my first book, mostly because I couldn't get out of my way. I worked in the IT department for 20 years. However, in 2017 I set a goal to start to write a book I'd begun writing a long time ago.

The desire to write this book was because I wanted to be able to help people have inner growth as I have done in the last ten years.

The problems had in the family, at work, and in everyday life, led me to make a path of growth myself. Seeing the significant improvements that I had, I felt the desire to write a book to give other people a starting point for a better quality of life.

I hope this book has given you some stimulus to start personal growth.

I would like you to be able to dedicate 5 minutes of your precious time to leave a review. The reviews are very important for me because I can understand what you think of my book. Receive valuable advice that will surely help me improve it.

Simply scan the QR code to be able to write your review directly.

Brandon Goleman

Table of Contents

References

Flasbeck, V., Enzi, B., & Brüne, M. (2019). Enhanced Processing of Painful Emotions in Patients With Borderline Personality Disorder: A Functional Magnetic Resonance Imaging Study. Frontiers In Psychiatry, 10. doi: 10.3389/fpsyt.2019.00357

Gerritsen, R., & Band, G. (2018). Breath of Life: The Respiratory Vagal Stimulation Model of Contemplative Activity. *Frontiers In Human Neuroscience, 12.* doi: 10.3389/fnhum.2018.00397

Harari, Y. (2019). *Sapiens*. London: Vintage.

Kasperkevic, J. (2014). Private Violence: up to 75% of abused women who are murdered are killed after they leave their partners. Retrieved 20 May 2020, from https://www.theguardian.com/money/us-money-blog/2014/oct/20/domestic-private-violence-women-men-abuse-hbo-ray-rice

Lo, I. (2018). The Unexpected Gifts Inside Borderline Personality. Retrieved 29 May 2020, from https://www.psychologytoday.com/us/blog/living-emotional-intensity/201805/the-unexpected-gifts-inside-borderline-personality

Mindtools. Emotional Intelligence in Leadership: Learning How to Be More Aware. Retrieved 20 May 2020, from https://www.mindtools.com/pages/article/newLDR_45.htm

n.a. (2019). Guns and Violence Against Women. Retrieved 20 May 2020, from https://everytownresearch.org/reports/guns-intimate-partner-violence/

Wagner, D. (2016). Polyvagal theory in practice - Counseling Today. Retrieved 20 May 2020, from https://ct.counseling.org/2016/06/polyvagal-theory-practice/

Empath

Brandon Goleman

A preview of Brandon Goleman's Emotional Intelligence book just for you...

Introduction

For the longest time, being smart and working hard were believed to be the perfect combination for success. Anybody who was not gifted in these two areas was viewed as having gotten the shorter end of the stick. People who scored well on intelligence quotient tests, or IQ scales, were seen to have an advantage over others when it came to succeeding in life. Even today, there are cultures and societies that believe that success is mutually inclusive with being book smart. Quite frankly, there is an advantage to being book smart. You will have an easier time going through school, you are more likely to get scholarships to help you with the financial cost of higher education, and you will generally have an easier time understanding concepts, be it in school or in life.

Unfortunately, book smarts can only get you so far. After paying attention to people who excelled in school and went on to be less successful than anticipated, psychologists have determined that there is something else required in this recipe for success. This extra ingredient is referred to as emotional intelligence. Emotional intelligence is not a concept that many people paid attention to until 1995. In that year, Daniel Goleman wrote about emotional intelligence in a book that popularized the term. Before then, the term had first appeared in a research paper written by Michael Beldoch. Beldoch was a psychologist at Cornell University. Between 1964 when Beldoch coined the term and 1995 when Goleman popularized it, other psychologists had written about emotional intelligence. However, there was not much attention paid to the concept. So, what changed that made people start paying attention?

Previously, researchers had mentioned emotional intelligence and even attempted to uncover what exactly it was. However, outside of research papers, there were not many written materials available for the general public to read. Goleman's book was really the first opportunity the world had to take an inside look at the world of emotional intelligence. At the same time, Goleman had built credibility working for the *New York Times* as a science writer. The fact that he was a Harvard-trained psychologist also helped his case. Goleman's book, *Emotional Intelligence,* remained on the *New York Times* bestseller list for one and a half years, a big feat by any standards. At the end of it all, the world had a new term that continues to be explored today.

What is emotional intelligence? In the simplest terms, emotional intelligence is the ability or skill to be intelligent about emotions. This includes your own emotions and those of others. If you take into consideration the various ways that emotional intelligence has been defined over the years, you might come up with other lengthier definitions such as:

Emotional quotient or EQ, which is the other name for emotional intelligence, is the ability to recognize, discern, and manage emotions.

Emotional intelligence, often abbreviated as EI, is the capacity to be cognizant and in control of one's emotions and to express these emotions appropriately. This skill extends from controlling your emotions internally when dealing with yourself and externally in interpersonal relationships.

Emotional intelligence means being able to pay attention to your emotions and the emotions of those around you while naming or labeling these correctly and to use the emotional information gathered from this exercise to respond appropriately.

There are endless ways in which you can define emotional intelligence, but the premise of it is this: Being emotionally intelligent means being aware of your emotions and using this heightened perception to manage yourself and other people as you go about life. Sometimes referred to as emotional quotient or emotional leadership, emotional intelligence comes in handy when your IQ cannot get the job done. How so?

Human beings are emotional creatures. In the course of a single day, we go through hundreds of emotions. Examples of emotions you might experience in a day include anger, sadness, joy, fear, disgust, and happiness. While scientists have not agreed on a standard definition of emotion, it is generally accepted that emotions are a state of mind. Emotions are triggered in the brain's limbic system. The limbic system is at the base of the brain and controls emotions by triggering a reaction from the endocrine system and the nervous system. The endocrine system is everything related to hormone production, while the nervous system relates to the network of nerves in your body. Simply put, the limbic brain prompts the endocrine and nervous systems to react based on the external stimuli that you are experiencing. If you are in a state of danger, the limbic system will sense that and interpret it appropriately, prompting the endocrine system to release adrenaline.

For the most part, human beings go through the same range of emotions, albeit at varying times. While your friend may be experiencing fear at the thought of skydiving, you might be feeling intense excitement. Later on, the roles might reverse when you are about to approach your crush while your friend looks on in anticipation. There are very few humans who are incapable of feeling emotions. Psychopaths, for instance, do not experience emotions as the average person would. Studies have been undertaken to show what the root cause of this is, with some psychologists explaining that the part of the brain capable of emotions is essentially broken when it comes to psychopaths.

That aside, the truth of the matter is that you will need to manage people and the different emotions that they bring with them more often than you'll need to rattle off the names of all the countries of the world and their capital cities. Few people care whether you can name the capital city of Monaco, but a whole lot of people care about how they feel after having a conversation with you. This is not to downplay the importance of being intelligent in other matters. Indeed, knowing how to read a map, among other things, will get you places, pun intended. But at the end of the day, reading people correctly and managing your emotional interactions with them will get you even further.

This book is your go-to handbook on all matters of emotional intelligence. It explains why emotions matter in everyday situations, it identifies all the opportunities that you have to apply emotional intelligence, and it helps you to test whether you have been acting intelligently as far as emotions are concerned. This book will show you how you can learn and practice emotional intelligence, even if you have not been very good at it in the past. If you are looking to improve your relationships in the workplace or at home, this is the only book you will ever have to read. The tips and tricks included inside can be adopted for any circumstance or environment. They are easy to execute, memorable, and even fun. At the end of the book, you'll realize that there is a whole lot of fulfillment to be gained from learning how to properly manage your emotions and those of others. A happier, easier, and more successful life awaits you at the end of the final chapter of this handbook.

Brandon Goleman 2020

Printed in Great Britain
by Amazon

38190614R00066